GEOMETRY

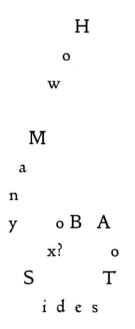

H
o
w

M
a
n
y   o B A
     x?   o
S   T
   i d e s

BOX

Henry Brown Mails Himself to Freedom

Carole Boston Weatherford

illustrated by Michele Wood

CANDLEWICK PRESS

I was born about forty-five miles from the city of Richmond, in Louisa County, in the year 1815. I entered the world a slave — in the midst of a country whose most honoured writings declare that all men have a right to liberty. . . . I was a slave because my countrymen had made it lawful, in utter contempt of the declared will of heaven, for the strong to lay hold of the weak and to buy and to sell them as marketable goods.

from *Narrative of the Life of Henry Box Brown, Written by Himself,* 1851

WIND

An autumn breeze blows maple leaves
While I sit on my mother's lap.
Slavery is a cruel wind, she says,
Sweeping children away from parents,
Scattering families far and wide.
She shivers and holds me close.

WORK

Like my seven sisters and brothers,
I am put to work as a child—
First serving my master and mistress,
Then learning plantation chores in the hot sun.
Every few months, I trudge twenty miles
With my brother, carrying grain to the mill.

BRUTALITY

Treks to market take my brother and me past plantations,

Where we encounter other blacks—some shoeless, coatless,

Nearly skin and bone in burlap shirts and threadbare pants.

We share our bread and meat with them. In the slave quarter,

They recount the savage beating that many of them got

For having been baptized just the night before.

SPLIT

I am fifteen when my master dies

And wills my family to his four sons,

My parents, brothers, sisters, and I

Flung apart as if dandelion puffs.

I land in the young master's Richmond tobacco factory.

He warns the overseer to never whip me.

RICHMOND

A sea of red brick rises from the James River,

Slavery the cornerstone of it all.

See the slave pens, whipping posts, auction houses.

Storefronts, tobacco factories, and gristmills—all busy.

Folks in packets and boats with cargo

Float along canals. People. Everywhere.

NAT

After three visions, enslaved preacher Nat Turner sees an eclipse as a sign.

He leads an army of forty-plus slaves to kill fifty-five whites.

Whites call them *monsters* and hang, knife, or shoot scores of slaves;

Others are whipped, put in irons, or half hanged and pelted with eggs.

Lawmakers pass stricter black codes but rule out ending slavery.

Nat Turner is tried, hanged, and skinned—but not before confessing.

FEAR

David Walker's *Appeal* called for slaves to rise up;

Nat Turner answered that call with rebellion. A massacre,

Whites called it. So scared that they raised the militia.

But slaves face fear every day: fear of the lash,

Of being sent farther south; fear of our families

Being sold off; fear of never, ever being free.

LAWS

Blacks may not carry canes, but must carry free papers or a slave pass.

Freed slaves must leave Virginia within a year or return to bondage.

No more than five blacks may gather, except in church.

Groups of blacks may worship only with a white preacher present.

It is unlawful to teach blacks to read and write.

Unwritten rule: As long as there is slavery, no blacks are safe.

OVERSEERS

When our black overseer dies, he is replaced by Stephen Bennett,

Whose peg leg won't let him sneak up to eavesdrop on the slaves.

He gives a hundred lashes for coming a few cents or pounds short on a task.

The next overseer, John F. Allen, is fiendish. When a slave who often sang

Takes sick, Allen has him dragged to the factory for two hundred lashes.

The whipping doesn't cease until the ailing man faints.

CROP

In March, sow tobacco seeds in plant beds.

Fertilize with fish meal. Late spring,

Transplant to the field. Plow row by row.

When the plants bloom, break off the tops.

Pull suckers from foliage so leaves will grow.

Late summer, split stalks three-quarters of the way down; cut plants above the ground.

CURING

One night in 1839, Stephen, an enslaved blacksmith on the Slade

Plantation in Caswell County, North Carolina, fell asleep.

In the log barn, he let the wood fires beneath the tobacco die.

He used charcoal to relight the fires. The tobacco leaves

Turned golden. Thus, brightleaf and flue-curing were born.

Stephen's master profited from the tobacco and the discovery.

PROCESSING

The brightleaf arrives by the barrel, by the cartload.

Strip stems from the tobacco;

Flavor leaves in cauldron of licorice and sugar.

Press into lumps and twist by hand.

In the machine house, pack into boxes and casks.

Lay in the sweat house for thirty days. Then sell.

NANCY

At work, days drag on like a long winter

Till I meet Nancy, an enslaved washerwoman

Whose laughter is the sweetest music I know.

To marry her, I need permission from her master.

He grants it; promises never ever to sell her,

Split us up. Me and my Nancy jump the broom.

FAMILY

Barely a year later, Nancy's master goes back on his word.

She and my children change hands like seasons,

Each master worse than the last. The last one, Mr. Cottrell, agrees

To keep my family if I feed them, house them, and pay him.

Small price, I figure. At First African Baptist Church, I join

The choir; thank God for keeping my family and faith intact.

WORTH

Nancy had been sold to Joseph Colquitt, a cruel saddler

With an even meaner wife. Mrs. Colquitt carped

That Nancy's breast-feeding and refined manners

Did not befit one enslaved. So her husband sold Nancy for $450.

Four months later, Mrs. Colquitt realized Nancy's worth

And begged her husband to buy her back. He did. For $500.

DEAL

A second saddler, Mr. Cottrell, told me that my wife's master,

Mr. Colquitt, aimed to sell her. Mr. Cottrell would step in

And buy her if I would chip in $50 of the $650 asking price

For Nancy and my children. He promised that if I did,

He would prevent her from being sold off.

To me, that seemed like a good bargain.

ANCHORED

The good Lord anchored me and Nancy in the Word

And has given us three children and, then, blessed news:

Another babe on its way in a matter of months.

Our family tree, my treasure, bears precious fruit.

Our harvest, though bountiful, yields a bitter truth:

We have less power to stay than weeds with shallow roots.

TRADE

Whites and blacks—enslaved and free—haggle in the marketplace,

Peddlers hawking eggs, chickens, potatoes, peas, and corn sticks.

Free blacks are barbers, blacksmiths, shoemakers

And shopkeepers, seamstresses and domestics.

They are allowed to buy land and own buildings.

If I had their money, I would buy my family.

RAILROAD

Richmond is not just a port city but also a railway hub.

Three lines converge: the Louisa Railroad,

The Richmond and Petersburg Railroad,

And the Richmond, Fredericksburg and Potomac Railroad.

I see the trains and imagine boarding one

Bound north, past the Mason-Dixon Line. Toward freedom.

MORE!

Nancy's master orders her to wash his clothes,

And me to stuff his pockets with silver.

I tell him, *None is due and I have none to spare.*

You will pay, he threatens, slamming a door.

As Nancy sobs, I hug her tight.

Our children flock around us, bracing against farewell.

SNATCHED

That very day, Nancy's master snatches

My family and pens them up for sale.

Robbed of all that matters, I beg my master's help.

But he gives me not one cent

Of my hard-earned wages that he's pocketed.

He says, *I dare not meddle.*

HELL

There's a reason that the slave jail at Shockoe Bottom

Is known as the Devil's Half Acre. Upstairs: the tavern

And boardinghouse run by bully trader Robert Lumpkin,

Who lives there with his slave wife, Mary. Downstairs:

A holding pen and a whipping room for breaking slaves.

I cannot bear the thought of my family locked inside.

TOKENS

I buy some tokens to take to my loved ones in jail,

Small sacrifice for one last embrace. On my way, a young man warns

That I might be jailed myself for lies that my master told the jailer.

The youth makes the delivery in my stead. But mistaken for me,

He is thrown in jail until my family's testimonies set him free.

The vexed jailer kicks the youth all the way into the street.

HEAVEN

For one last glimpse of my loved ones, I watch

The slave chain pass, bound for North Carolina.

Father! Father! my child yells from a wagon.

I see my wife, grab her hand, and walk four miles with her.

We shall meet in heaven, I whisper. Then she is gone.

Lord, what more have I to lose?

FRIENDS

When I needed a freeman to enter a contract for me
So that I could rent a house for my family,
James Caesar Anthony Smith signed his name.
When I needed money to pay Mr. Cottrell's debt
And collect my household goods before auction,
Dr. Smith had the remedy: seventeen dollars.

CHURCH

Leaning on God, I sing at church with my friend
Dr. Smith. After several hymns, he kneels and sobs,
The sin of human bondage suddenly clear to him.
He vows never to worship at another church
That twists the bible to uphold slavery.
I, too, need to take a strong stance.

U.G.R.R.

I have heard whispers of a way
That is neither underground nor a railroad,
Yet it goes by that name, though only in hushed tones.
Secret routes, safe houses, songs of stealing away.
In those songs, I hear a yearning—
The same longing in my soul.

PLAN

From that day on, I ponder escape. But how—
With only $166 to my name?
While I'm at work, prayer shows me the way.
I pay a carpenter to build a wooden box:
Two feet deep, three feet wide, and two and a half feet long.
I drill three holes in the box. For air.

COURAGE

What have I to fear?

My master broke every promise to me.

I lost my beloved wife and our dear children.

All sold south. Neither my time nor my body is mine.

The breath of life is all I have to lose.

And bondage is suffocating me.

HELP

I have a plan, a box, and a strong resolve,

But I cannot pull off the escape alone.

I need an accomplice to close the lid

And a traveling companion to keep the crate upright.

I offer to pay Samuel Smith, a trusted shoemaker.

He doubts I can survive the trip but agrees to go with me.

LETTER

Dear Mr. McKim,

We applaud your righteous abolitionist work.

We humbly request your help in a daring mission to deliver

A slave to freedom as freight. We would be grateful

If you will agree to receive the box.

Respectfully, Mr. Samuel Smith.

EXCUSE

If I miss work without permission, that will spark suspicion.

I need a few days off with permission to fool my master.

The overseer examines my hurt finger but denies me leave—

Until I pour acid on the wound to make it worse.

This time, the overseer glimpses bone. He is convinced.

This sore is my head start to liberty.

MANIFEST

Inside

One

Box

To

Flee

Another.

INSIDE

I take a bladder of water and a drill to bore air holes
And cram my two-hundred-pound body into the box.
Samuel Smith and James Smith nail my box shut.
Inside, I feel the hammering.
They mark the box PHILADELPHIA—THIS SIDE UP
And hope I can pass as dry goods.

BAGGAGE

The Smiths send my box to Adams Express,
Where I am turned upside down, loaded
Onto a wagon, and driven to the train depot.
A man tumbles me into the baggage car,
And I fall on my right side.
My heart races as the train chugs away.

SWEAT

At Potomac Creek, my box is moved
To a steamer and again placed upside down.
My eyes bulge, my veins swell, until I break a sweat.
Then two travelers knock my box over to sit on it.
I wonder what's inside, one man says.
The mail, the other replies.

OUCH!

In Washington, I am carted, right side up,
From the steamboat to the train depot.
This box must be full of lead, a man says,
Shoving me from the wagon.
I land upside down and my neck cracks.
I black out from the pain.

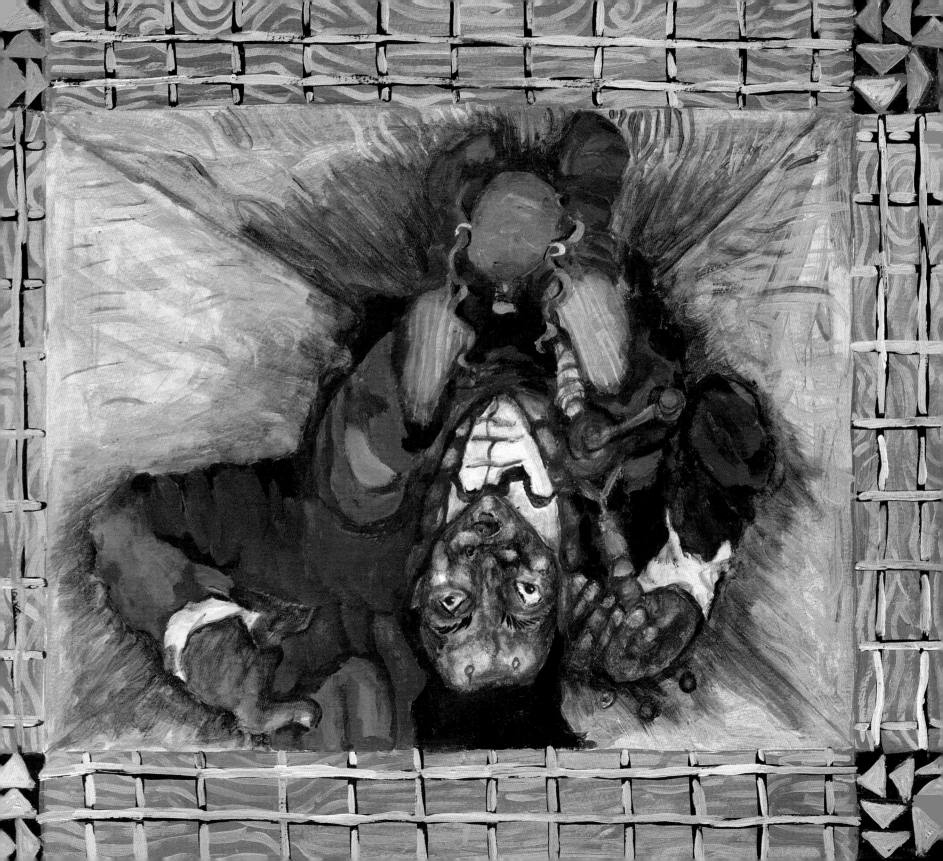

EXPRESS

When I awaken, two men are debating
Whether there is room on board for my box.
It will have to sit here till tomorrow, says one man.
It came express, says another. *It has to go now.*
I am put on the train upside down but get shifted
Onto my right side. Still, my limbs cramp.

WAIT

Twenty-seven hours, 350 miles.
Philadelphia! a voice bellows.
I wait, but the friend I'd paid does not come.
Hours pass, and no one greets me.
I pray this crate will not be my coffin.
That evening, a man claims my box.

FREE

After a short wagon ride, I am lugged inside.

Folks gather around. I keep quiet.

What did the telegraph say? a man asks.

Someone raps on the lid. *Is all right within?*

All right, I reply. They pry open the lid,

And I step out a free man. I burst into song.

Anti-Slavery Office
Phila., March 26 /49

Dear Gay,

Here is a man who has been the hero of one of
the most extraordinary achievements I ever heard
of. He came to me on Saturday morning last in a
box tightly hooped, marked "this side up" by over-
land express, from the city of Richmond!! Did
you ever hear of any thing in your life to beat
that? . . . It was a regular old store box . . . grooved
at the joints and braced at the ends, leaving but
the very slightest crevice to admit the air. Nothing
saved him from suffocation but the free use of water
. . . and the constant fanning of himself with his
hat. . . . The "this side up" on the box was not
regarded, and he was twice put with his head down-
wards—resting with his back against the end of the
box, his feet braced against the other. . . . The
second time was on board the steamboat. . . . This
nearly killed him. He says the veins in his temples
were as thick as his finger.

  I had been expecting him for several days,
and was in mortal fear all the time lest his
arrival should only be a signal for calling the
coroner. . . . He will tell you the whole
story. . . .

  Don't publish this affair or allow it to be
published. It would compromise the Express, and prevent all others from escaping in the same way.

Yours truly
J.M. McKim

"BOX"

At the New England Anti-Slavery Convention, I sing the hymn
That was on my lips when I first breathed liberty.
Touring anti-slavery gatherings, I tell my story
And hawk my song lyrics and new book.
For abolitionists, I am tangible proof that the enslaved
Crave freedom. I earn the nickname "Box."

PRICE

Even if I could find my family, I would need $1,000
Or more to buy a woman and four children out of slavery.
Saving that much could take the rest of my days—
If I could elude bounty hunters that long.
My family would have to flee to Canada or risk capture.
A dark shadow of helplessness looms over me.

SLEEPLESS

Is my beloved, my Nancy, still with our children,
Or have they been sold again, sold apart perhaps?
Whom can I ask to write letters, make inquiries?
If I could raise enough money to buy my family's freedom,
Whom could I trust with the transaction?
If I never see them again, how will I press on?

MIRROR

Convinced that my saga must be seen to be believed,

I enlist a Boston artist to create a moving panorama,

A backdrop of massive paintings in the round.

Henry Box Brown's Mirror of Slavery tours New England,

And spectators immerse themselves in the very institution I fled.

I reenact my unboxing, complete with a replica of the crate.

FUGITIVE

In Providence, Rhode Island, I am attacked on the street—

A kidnapping plot, I suspect, to return me to Richmond.

Soon after, the Fugitive Slave Bill becomes law.

Boston is crawling with bounty hunters. Price on my head,

I sail to England with my panorama and my pain-filled past.

Across the Atlantic, I begin to build a new life.

ENGLAND

My panorama tours Liverpool, Manchester, Lancashire, and Yorkshire.

Then money squabbles lead my partner, James Smith, to write

Abolitionists complaining that I have not tried to buy back my family.

How would I find them? And whom could I trust to liberate them?

Not a day passes that I do not long for my dear wife and children.

Yet my anti-slavery work is now stained.

NEWS

In England, news reaches me of one Anthony Burns,

An enslaved preacher who fled Richmond for Boston at age nineteen.

In 1854, he is captured and tried under the Fugitive Slave Act.

A riot leaves a U.S. marshal dead. Back down south,

Burns is jailed at the Devil's Half Acre and obtains a bible

From Lumpkin's slave wife. Abolitionists buy his freedom.

SHOWMAN

Just as my escape transformed me into a freeman,

I reinvent myself onstage. For my one-man show,

I cast a new character, a well-dressed African prince.

Later, I spice up my act with hypnotism.

Audiences laugh at volunteers under my spell.

I crown myself "King of all the Mesmerisers."

MAGICIAN

My new life brings a second chance for happiness.

I remarry and we have a daughter. I take them home.

In the United States, I call myself Professor H. Box Brown.

I perform magic tricks, but still portray the African prince

And climb from the box that delivered me to freedom.

After all, my escape was my finest illusion.

AXIOM

Freedom
Is
Fragile.
Handle
With
Care.

TIME LINE

1815 or 1816
Henry Brown is born enslaved in Louisa County, Virginia. He is owned by John Barret, a former mayor of Richmond.

1822
Denmark Vesey is arrested, tried, and executed for planning a massive slave revolt in South Carolina.

1830
After the death of their master, fifteen-year-old Henry's family is split up. Henry is relocated to Richmond to work in a tobacco factory.

1831
AUGUST: Spurred on by religious visions, Nat Turner, an enslaved Baptist preacher, leads a slave rebellion.

1833
Great Britain abolishes slavery in all of its colonies, effective the following year. The American Anti-Slavery Society is established in Philadelphia.

1839
Fifty-three African captives on board the slave ship *Amistad* revolt and mutiny. In resulting trials, they are acquitted, and the thirty-five surviving former captives return to Sierra Leone.

1848
While Henry's wife, Nancy, is pregnant with their fourth child, she and their children are sold away to a plantation in North Carolina.

1849
MARCH 23–24: Samuel A. Smith ships Henry Brown in a wooden box to the Philadelphia headquarters of the Anti-Slavery Society.

Harriet Tubman escapes from slavery in Maryland. She will go on to become a leader of the Underground Railroad, helping countless slaves escape to freedom.

MAY 8: After attempting to ship more enslaved people from Virginia to Pennsylvania, Samuel A. Smith is discovered and arrested.

The Narrative of the Life of Henry Box Brown is published in Boston by Charles Stearns.

1850

Brown premieres a moving panorama entitled "Mirror of Slavery" in Boston.

SEPTEMBER 18: The Fugitive Slave Act of 1850 is enacted. It requires that all escaped slaves be returned to their owners and that government officials and citizens assist in that process. It creates risks for those escaping slavery, as well as for those helping them, and even threatens the status of free blacks.

Fearing capture, Brown sails to England and begins exhibiting his panorama there.

1851

The Narrative of the Life of Henry Box Brown, Written by Himself, is published in England.

1857

MARCH 6: In its decision on *Dred Scott v. Sandford,* the United States Supreme Court rules that African Americans are not entitled to national citizenship and that Congress cannot exclude slavery from new territories.

1859

Jane Floyd becomes Henry's second wife.

OCTOBER 16: In Harpers Ferry, Virginia, abolitionist John Brown leads a small band of men in an unsuccessful attempt to launch an insurrection against slavery.

1860

NOVEMBER 6: Abraham Lincoln is elected the sixteenth president of the United States.

1861

FEBRUARY 18: Jefferson Davis is sworn in as president of the Confederate States.

APRIL 12: The Civil War begins with the Confederate attack on Fort Sumter, in Charleston, South Carolina.

1863

JANUARY 1: Lincoln issues the Emancipation Proclamation, freeing all slaves in the areas of rebellion.

1865

APRIL 14: Lincoln is shot and dies the next day.

MAY 9: The Civil War ends when Confederate general Robert E. Lee surrenders to U.S. general Ulysses S. Grant at Appomattox Court House, Virginia.

DECEMBER 6: The Thirteenth Amendment to the Constitution, abolishing slavery in the United States, is ratified.

Southern states begin to pass Black Codes, restricting the newfound freedoms of ex-slaves.

1870

The Fifteenth Amendment to the Constitution, prohibiting the state from denying citizens the right to vote on the basis of race, is ratified.

1875

Henry "Box" Brown returns to America with his wife, Jane, and daughter Annie.

1889

FEBRUARY 26: Brown's last documented performance takes place in Ontario, Canada.

1896

The Supreme Court rules in *Plessy v. Ferguson* that segregation is constitutional as long as separate establishments are "equal." The decision paves the way for legalized segregation.

1897

JUNE 15: Henry "Box" Brown dies in Toronto.

BIBLIOGRAPHY

Africans in America. "The *Richmond Enquirer* on Nat Turner's Rebellion." "The Banditti."
Richmond (VA) *Enquirer.* April 30, 1831. WGBH/PBS Online. http://www.pbs.org/wgbh/aia
/part3/3h499t.html.

Brown, Henry "Box." *Narrative of the Life of Henry Box Brown, Written by Himself.* Manchester,
England: Lee and Glynn, 1851. Documenting the American South. University of North Carolina at
Chapel Hill. http://docsouth.unc.edu/neh/brownbox/brownbox.html.

Cowan, Alison Leigh. "When Special Delivery Meant Deliverance for a Fugitive Slave."
City Room (blog). *New York Times.* February 26, 2010. https://cityroom.blogs.nytimes.com
/2010/02/26/when-special-delivery-meant-deliverance-for-a-fugitive-slave/.

Still, William. *The Underground Railroad: A Record of Fact, Authentic Narratives, Letters, Etc.*
Philadelphia: People's Publishing Company, 1871.

Turner, Nat. *The Confessions of Nat Turner, The Leader of the Late Insurrection in Southampton,
VA.* Baltimore: Thomas R. Gray, 1831. *Documenting the American South.* University of North
Carolina at Chapel Hill. http://docsouth.unc.edu/neh/turner/turner.html.

A NOTE FROM THE ILLUSTRATOR

The text of this book is impactful all on its own. The poems are rich, insightful, and informative and dance to a song of beauty and suffering. My hope in creating illustrations for them was to do so in a way that maintained their dignity and integrity. I needed to convey the deep suffering of poems such as "Brutality" and "Split." The palette I chose includes blue, green, pink, red, and neutrals, which are colors of the 1800s. And I also wanted to unfold the levels of hope and determination I felt in Henry Brown's story and to display Henry's gratefulness. Oh, how he was grateful to the Lord for his survival and that he was free from bondage.

A special thank-you to the members of my focus group: former special education teacher Dorothy Zeis; retired seminary professor Dr. Rev. Carol Johnston; dean of libraries at Butler University, Dr. Julie Miller; associate curator of social history at the Indiana State Museum, Kisha Tandy; and executive director of the Center for Interfaith Cooperation, Charlie Wiles, and his daughter, Mia.

A NOTE ON NUMBERS AND LANGUAGE

Reflecting the cubic structure of a box, the number six figures prominently in this book's text. All but one of the poems are sixains, having six lines. (The one nonconformer is the opening concrete poem, "Geometry," which has six words and forms a numeral 6.)

Box: Henry Brown Mails Himself to Freedom is a true account retold in first-person poems. To re-create Henry Box Brown's voice and a sense of the language of the day, I referred to his narrative. I also read texts by David Walker, Nat Turner, and Frederick Douglass, who knew slavery firsthand. These African-American abolitionists used terms such as *slave, black,* and *Negro.* Nowadays, the term *enslaved person* is preferred to *slave.* In these poems, I use old and new terms interchangeably. That is how I reconcile a nineteenth-century voice with twenty-first-century thought. After all, no words can fully fathom slavery's inhumanity.

In memory of the Underground Railroad and
all those who toiled or traveled on it in secrecy
C. B. W.

I dedicate this book to the kids I have come to know: Mia, Christian, Angel, Gabby,
Dylin, Davarie, Jlin, Mikale, Marcelo, and Juliana. Your gifts are to be treasured.
"For where your treasure is, there your heart will be also" (Matthew 6:21).
M. W.

Text copyright © 2020 by Carole Boston Weatherford
Illustrations copyright © 2020 by Michele Wood

First edition 2020

Library of Congress Catalog Card Number pending
ISBN 978-0-7636-9156-1

20 21 22 23 24 25 LEO 10 9 8 7 6 5 4 3 2 1

Printed in Heshan, Guangdong, China

This book was typeset in Golden Type.
The illustrations were done in mixed media.

Candlewick Press
99 Dover Street
Somerville, Massachusetts 02144

visit us at www.candlewick.com